The poetry fair

The fair of 28 interesting poems.

The Ankit Kumar Gaur

ISBN 978-93-5458-783-2

© The Ankit Kumar Gaur 2021

Published in India 2021 by Pencil

A brand of

One Point Six Technologies Pvt. Ltd.

123, Building J2, Shram Seva Premises,

Wadala Truck Terminal, Wadala (E)

Mumbai 400037, Maharashtra, INDIA

E connect@thepencilapp.com

W www.thepencilapp.com

CONTENTS

About the book

This book is a combination of poetries based on love, loneliness, inspiration and reality. This book is mainly divided into four parts.

Each part has its own value and introduces us to different types of poetry. Every poem is different from each other and trying to entertain us.

In the first part we will find ten poems dedicated to love, in the second and third parts we will find eight poems each dedicated to inspiration and loneliness. Finally in the fourth part we will find two poems dedicated to reality. In this book the author is trying to entertain us through poetry. I hope you all will enjoy the book.

Poem-1. Meet you.

Often being a little selfish,

I pray this from my heart.

Whenever I pass by the way,

I want your presence in the way.

I wish this happens someday,

I will go on the way and meet you.

How beautiful will that moment be,

The day I will be with you.

Now I talk about you often,

Now I just want to meet you.

I wish someday where this happiness showers on me like this,

I will go on the way and meet you.

You meet - then I want to talk a lot,

Things that are left unfinished.

I want your support to fulfil them,

I wish this happens in my life,

I get up whenever my eyes get to see your face.

I wish every moment of mine could be yours,

I will go on the way, and meet you.

The right to call you my own - I want to ask from the world,

I admit I have never mentioned it, but I have started loving you.

I don't know when this happened,

Maybe I can say I have been yours for a few days.

I wish I could be with you wherever I am

I will go on the way - and meet you.

Whenever I talk - I want to mention you in the talk,

Whenever I am alone - I want your presence in loneliness.

Talk about anything - I want to mention you in those things,

I have become yours - I want to hear these words from you.

I wish that your name should be written on my every breath,

I will go on the way - and meet you.

I wish it was like this - every moment is mine, with you,

Whatever sorrow is there - you are with me in that moment.

Even if the lines in the hands are not the same,

But you are near me - every moment of mine is just beginning with you.

I wish both of us could be for each other's forever,

I will walk on the way - and meet you.

I wish we both have a relationship.

I will walk on the way - and meet you.

Poem-2 Something is happening to me now

What shall I say, what shall I not say?

What will I talk about, what will I not do?

If I said something, what would she understand?

Will the friendship last or grow?

Will she say yes or not?

Will talk or end the story.

Now the mind is getting lost in this thought,

Looks like something is happening to me now.

Now I will also dive in the ocean of love,

Now I will pray more for her life.

I will include her in every dream,

The talk will be half but I will do it complete.

Now I will spend more time on it,

While she said anything or not - I will understand everything about her by heart.

Now all the time this mind has started making up the same things,

Looks like something is happening to me now.

Sometimes I'll cry! Sometimes she'll cry,

I would say sometime! Sometimes she will say.

I'll make him laugh sometime! Sometimes she will make me laugh,

Seeing this, years will pass by.

There will be laughter every moment of the day,

There will be confusion between the two.

Happiness has started coming in my life too,

Looks like something is happening to me now.

I don't know what she will say! When I talk her heartfelt words,

She will also say something from her heart or she will remain silent.

I don't know what is going to happen now,

Looks like I'm going to find someone of my own.

Will talk to eyes - will meet in dreams,

Would be a bit surprised! There will be some simplicity.

My thoughts have started descending in her heart too.

Looks like something is happening to me now.

Nowadays I sleep less, eyes have started waking up more,

Want to meet her! But my heart has stopped beating.

I want to sit beside her - but there is a strange stir in my heart,

I want to say that I have started loving her! But the tongue has stopped in front of her.

I want to say the matter of my heart but I do not have the courage to say it,

I am wondering what will she do.

Now the eyes are just waiting for his arrival,

Looks like something is happening to me now.

Give her a hug! I will keep heart in my heart,

Let me add my name to her name.

If she says yes, I will settle the world with her,

Heart is starting to feel his breath.

Looks like something is happening to me now.

The heart has started insisting thousands to get him,

Looks like something is happening to me now.

POEM-3 I am getting lost in your intoxication.

People say that I have become crazy,

I know what I'm saying.

I am talking about myself as I say,

Writing to you is not my hobby, it is my art.

I am making everyone realize this,

It seems that I am getting lost in your intoxication.

How can I say How grateful I am to your?

It is because of you that my name has emerged.

Now I have started writing your own words,

Was made for you, now I have started meeting you only.

I do not say that I have started doing something new,

It seems that I am getting lost in your intoxication.

I have started writing - I have started reading you,

I have started spending the day behind you.

I have made the world my own in you,

I have started spending my life in you.

I'm starting to feel you,

It seems that I am getting lost in your intoxication.

How can I say that you have a lot of favour on me,

I have made my name out of you only.

Praying that you never leave my side,

Support me till I die.

I have become despondent on being you,

It seems that I am getting lost in your intoxication.

You have become my purpose,

You have become a breath to live.

I would not like to be separated from you for a moment,

Nor will I tolerate separation from you.

Well I can call you mine,

It seems that I am getting lost in your intoxication.

Now you have become a habit,

Looks like you have become important to me.

What would I be without you,

I will be lonely without you.

Every story of mine starts with you,

You have to come by writing in my every word.

I talk about everything with the help of you,

It seems that I am getting lost in your intoxication.

Starting my day with you only,

It seems that I am getting lost in your intoxication.

POEM-4 This life of mine is now only yours.

Believe me, I have become yours,

I do not wish for anything other than you.

Told you my own! I will not call any other my own,

Now I'll be yours.

Tell me yours,

Sit next to me for a while.

Don't stay away now! This distance of ours is going to end now,

This life of mine is now only yours.

Since yours! Since than I have completed,

Had to meet every-day in dreams.

Often you had to add to things,

I think now I am yours.

This life of mine is pleasant with you,

Looks like happiness is about to come in my life.

I have nothing in me now,

This life of mine is now only yours.

Because of your smile, this life of mine has started smiling,

A new beginning is about to start in my life.

How can I tell you, all my things are yours,

Now it's time to start life with you.

I want to call you mine,

I'll make you mine I will make a relation with you.

Now it's my turn to come to your memories,

This life of mine is now only yours.

I wish I could join you in every moment,

I can call you mine in front of everyone.

Give me this right! I just want this order from you,

Now my every prayer has to be accepted from you only.

I want to see you when I wake up

I want you with me as soon as I open my eyes.

Every morning of mine is going to start with you now,

This life of mine is now only yours.

Put me in your eyes,

You come in my life as happiness.

How long will you remain a stranger to me?

How long will you keep hiding things from me?

Now tell me everything about you,

Now my own.

Now the life of both of us is going to be one,

This life of mine is now only yours.

It seems that now you are mine

This life of mine is now only yours.

POEM-5 It seems that now this heart is not my own.

There is a strange movement in the heart,

I don't know what he wants.

Neither does it keep itself calm, nor does it allow me to remain calm,

I don't know what's going on! Don't know what he wants to say.

Nowadays this heart does not hear anything,

It seems that now this heart is not my own.

Walked a lot alone,

Now the feet ask for someone's support.

The eyes have seen many,

Now the eyes want your sight.

Now the heartbeat has started beating in your name,

It seems that now this heart is not my own.

I don't know what I'm thinking today,

I myself started talking.

I have started falling in love with life now,

This heart is starting to do something bad.

Now I don't need anyone except you,

It seems that now this heart is not my own.

I think what am I doing,

I'm thinking of you I have started loving you.

There's a bit of confusion! There's a little silence,

A little movement has started happening in the heart.

Now I have no relation with the world,

It seems that now this heart is not my own.

Nowadays eyes are looking for you

Now this sleep of mine has started becoming yours

Tell yourself less! I want to hear you more

Whatever the distance between us! Now I want to erase all.

Now this day I don't feel complete,

It seems that now this heart is not my own.

21

Now this heart is looking for your support,

I have started spending the whole day remembering you.

This world of mine is not complete in me,

I am feeling the need of you now.

Now I don't like any moment,

It seems that now this heart is not my own.

Now the heart does not agree to be apart from you,

It seems that now this heart is not my own.

POEM-6 Feeling you in my heartbeat now.

I have started living apart from myself.

There is a little loneliness in the heart,

I am frightened by the slightest movement in my heart.

Silence seems to be around,

I am frightened by the movement around.

The heart has hidden something,

I have started feeling you in my heartbeat now.

I'm thinking of what to say

I am near you - I want to be near you.

Heart says! Let me tell you everything,

I will spend the rest of my life with you.

Now the distance between us,

I want to erase that distance forever.

I don't know why I am getting upset.

I have started feeling you in my heartbeat now.

Now call me yours for a moment,

Say whatever you want to say.

How long will I live in the hope of calling you my own,

How long will I be happy to see you away?

Now let's move on,

Joins life together for each other.

Now I want to start my every day with you,

I am now feeling you in my heartbeat.

I don't like anything nowadays,

If I stay with you, I don't know the time.

Now I have started seeing my life in you,

How can I tell you I have become yours.

Let's sit with each other someday,

Talks a lot with each other.

Nowadays I am fond of listening to your voice,

I am now feeling you in my heartbeat.

Now you join me in every moment,

To be mine - steal me from me.

You join me in every morning,

stay with me! Make my every moment yours.

Want to say something! feel free to tell me,

Tell me a little, listen to me a little.

Now I have started finding the day incomplete without you,

I have started feeling you in my heartbeat now.

Nowadays I am starting to find myself alone.

I can feel you in my heartbeat now.

POEM-7 It seems that slowly I am becoming yours.

Today, saw you passing through my street,

It felt as if a traveller had got his sight.

Keep watching you - keep feeling your presence,

Thought I would bring you here - let me introduce you to the people of the house.

Then thought I'm not doing it in a hurry,

It seems that slowly I am becoming yours.

I remember! You never called me yours,

But the heart is still waiting to make you my own.

When I saw you for the first time! Since than I have made you my own,

Was just waiting for your one word.

I felt that what ever happened to me - the same is happening to you too,

Heart is beating here, in your name! So maybe you have started feeling that feeling too.

Hardly I am living for myself now,

It seems that slowly I am becoming yours.

Every-day I have always been happy just seeing you with my eyes ,

Neither could I say anything to you nor could I tell my pain to you.

I was always a stranger even after being near you,

Wanted to say so many times! But the words did not support.

Now I am making you the support of my life,

It seems that slowly I am becoming yours.

There is one thing in my heart that I have to say to you,

Now every story of mine has to begin with you.

Feeling something new is happening,

I feel happy every moment with you.

Don't leave me alone on the way of life

Don't prove my decision wrong.

I am dreaming of spending my life with you,

It seems that slowly I am becoming yours.

Have to make your own! I want to spend every moment with you,

Have to be happy! I have to become the reason for that happiness.

I want to be a part of your every moment,

I want to spend the journey of life with you.

One has said only to you! I am no longer concerned with others,

It seems that slowly I am becoming yours.

Eyes wish to see you,

The desire of the heart is to be yours.

Waiting for my every moment, now it's only yours,

You just have to keep your hand in the hands.

Before I say anything, I have to understand everything about you,

I want to come in your sleep.

Now I am adding you to my every wish,

It seems that slowly I am becoming yours.

POEM-8 Now I'm starting to miss you.

I've got a new reason to live,

Life has become better after meeting you.

Now my eyes have become used to seeing you,

I met you! Since than you have become my reality.

Now you have started being involved in this heartbeat

Now I'm starting to miss you.

Wherever I go! I am meeting you now,

The tongue is filling your name all the time.

If God is in the world,

So having found you, God's mercy has showered on me.

Eyes now want to see this dream of yours,

Now I'm starting to miss you.

What am I doing wrong that I want to be yours,

With you, I am only wishing for you now.

What am I doing wrong, I want to call you my own,

Had asked for a prayer from God! Having found you, I am able to fulfil my prayers.

Now you have become like a habit of mine,

Now I'm starting to miss you.

Now call me yours too

Why do you keep silent? Say something,

The heart remains restless to hear your words,

Give up hope of finding you! Its heart does not approve.

Now the heartbeat has started coming from your name,

Now I'm starting to miss you.

Now I don't want to stay away from you!

Stay away from you, there is no reason between us now.

I know you love me too,

We have come often in your dreams.

I'm restless! Now sleep has started opening with your voice,

Now I'm starting to miss you.

Sit next to me for a while! I have something to say,

Things that have been incomplete for a long time!

They have to do it.

Now I am starting to feel incomplete in me,

Whenever I'm alone I'm starting to feel you.

My path is now looking for you,

Now I'm starting to miss you.

POEM-9 Beginning of my day, become you now.

There is a dream in the eyes,There

In making dreams a reality! You be my side.

Some relationships have to be performed, till those relationships are fulfilled,

You become my support.

I want to live happily every day,

Beginning of my day, become you now.

There is something missing in life without you,

Every story of mine is incomplete now.

I want to meet you now,

I want to live every moment with you.

Be me you are involved in every moment,

Beginning of my day, become you now.

You don't even know! To what extent have I started loving you,

I have started seeing myself with you.

I have started understanding your every dream as my own,

I have started connecting myself with you.

You become the reality of my every day,

Beginning of my day, become you now.

Whenever I wake up want you near

Keep watching you! I want to steal that moment from the world.

I am starting to feel you! I want to make you my reality

You don't have to remember me! I want to join your destiny.

Be me forever, now you remain,

Beginning of my day, become you now.

I am waiting for that day,

The day I will be yours.

I'll start my day with you,

I will be with you by making you my companion.

Now become the means of erasing my loneliness,

Beginning of my day, become you now.

Have something to say to you I want to hear something
from you,

What is lacking in our relationship right now I want to
remove that deficiency.

Now whenever I close my eyes I have started seeing

you in my dreams,

Now you have become my need to live.

Be with me every moment,

Beginning of my day, become you now.

POEM-10 The distance between us is now getting shorter.

Words will fall short if I sit to tell his story,

A little smart, a little naughty, a little innocent.

There is enough anger on his lips but there is a lot of truth in the heart,

Whenever she meets me I think what to say.

There is a slight confusion but one thing that seems to be clear to me

The distance between us is now getting shorter.

She has started calling me hers nowadays, she has started giving me her time,

She is starting to make me feel a little special.

She has started settling me in her eyes,

The world is different for both of them, but now she has started connecting them with each other.

She has started laughing herself, now she has started laughing with me, never said but now she has started explaining to me in gestures,

The distance between us is now getting shorter.

No matter how much you talk, the talk never ends,

I start seeing something new every-day.

Suddenly gets lost somewhere, spoils all the work,

Then apologizes to me and gets lost back in her fun.

Many times, I think I should give him a slap but her smile solves all the problems,

The distance between us is now getting shorter.

Now it seems to me that she wants to understand,

She likes to walk with me these days.

Earlier she was a little hesitant now she has started telling me everything,

I don't talk much but I have to talk to him thousands.

Now it is starting to become the colour of the season,

The distance between us is now getting shorter.

Now she wants to see me with her and wants to be associated with me forever,

Now she wants to see my name associated with her.

She comes to meet me at night hiding from everyone,

Then come and wake me up slowly.

Shows too much haste,

The distance between us is now getting shorter.

Finally both of us are becoming one, today we are being done in the name of each other,

The happiness of both of them has not been soft today.

Now she has started bothering me a bit, now she is making me happy,

Everyone has started fighting for me, my new job is now to pacify her.

Her arrival has added happiness to my life,

The distance between us is now getting shorter.

Part-2. Poem dedicated to loneliness.

Poem-1 I'm lonely here! Come and hug me.

I admit I could never say,

The condition of the heart could not be expressed.

It's been a long time since I talked to you,

Many days have passed! Hear your voice.

It seems this world is broken,

I have lost my happiness.

I agree, I have never brought the matter of my heart on my tongue,

I'm lonely here! Come and hug me.

What should I complain to someone,

Now I am complaining to myself.

Didn't recognize you when you were near,

Couldn't recognize your love by staying with you.

I want to sit with you again,

Listen, I want to talk to you about something.

Now I can't miss a moment without you,

I'm lonely here! Come and hug me.

Your that look at me - tell me to look good,

Tell me to stay with me.

Listen carefully to everything I say,

was crazy! Who doesn't know your love.

I want to hear you now! I want to live life with you again,

I want you to call me yours again! Fill my life with happiness again.

I don't want to stay away from you for a moment,

I'm lonely here! Come and hug me.

Remember You told me how cute I am,

No one can call me cute without you.

I know I have hurt you,

I made you dead while alive.

Now I am thinking - once again to make a new life with you,

All those laughter moments with you, to be alive again.

Give me the right to call you my own again,

I'm lonely here! Come and hug me.

Now I want to talk to you again,

I want to hear your voice again.

Give me one more chance,

Make my life beautiful again.

I know it will not be so easy for you,

To revive our spoiled life.

Try once for our relationship,

I'm lonely here! Come and hug me.

Let's once again hold each other's hand,

Forget everything and start again.

Now there will be no complaint with each other,

Life will be settled again with happiness.

I am ready for a new beginning with you,

To put my every moment behind you again.

Now come and look at me with love again

I'm lonely here! Come and hug me.

41

Start another new life with me again,

I'm lonely here! Come and hug me.

Poem-2 It is not even written in life.

I will hardly be able to meet you now,

I can hardly call you my own.

Don't know when we will get together again,

Don't know when we will ask each other's condition again.

I don't think we will ever be able to talk on the phone now,

Looks like there will be some distance between us now.

Maybe our love is not approved by God,

Perhaps the life of both of us is related to each other, it is not even written in life.

We'll never be able to hang out together again,

Neither will they be able to talk sweetly to each other.

Now you don't want to touch me as yours

Nor would you like to tell me your pain.

You will no longer be in my memories,

Nor will I be yours anymore.

Now I will not see that smile of yours again,

Perhaps the life of both of us is related to each other, it is not even written in life.

Now you will always look at me with a stranger's eye,

You will never be able to see yourself in my eyes.

How am I, I am fine, whenever you see me, this is what you would like to ask,

But there will also be your family with you, so even if you want, you will not ask me anything.

Looks like we were together till this time,

This was the relation of the lines of the hands.

Now again we will not be able to enjoy being near each other,

Perhaps the life of both of us is related to each other, it is not even written in life.

Now you will not be able to openly ask me anything,

Now after seeing me on the road, you won't tell me yes like before.

Won't you say are you sad today,

Won't you ask me is there any problem.

You will only be troubled by yourself,

You will find your happiness in someone else's happiness.

Now you will not have to meet secretly in the night,

Perhaps the life of both of us is related to each other, it is not even written in life.

Looks like now we have to live by staying away,

Now even after seeing each other, we both have to remain ignorant.

Whenever you come near, now you have to keep yourself apart.

Sometimes the way will be found! But both of us still have to live in the unconsciousness.

Now we won't be able to laugh together again,

Neither will they be able to see each other for the rest of their lives.

Now we will not be of each other,

Perhaps the life of both of us is related to each other, it is not even written in life.

Maybe you ask me sometime how are you

I will say, I am fine and then I will ask how are you.

You might also say the same

But know it will be something else.

Maybe we'll meet again somewhere

I hope you don't think of me as a stranger.

How will I live without you, have you never thought this,

Perhaps the life of both of us is related to each other, it is not even written in life.

Now there is no support for you in the nights, now my eyes have no relief for you,

Perhaps the life of both of us is related to each other, it is not even written in life.

POEM-3 I have got a reason not to live.

I am little tired now I am broken

It seems that life has become angry with me, now this fate has troubled me.

I don't feel like talking to anyone anymore.

Because loneliness has made me friends.

Eyes are getting tired now

Because now I have got a reason not to live.

A little bad time is going on today so I am sitting alone,

Everything is going on in the way but I have to spend my life alone in some corner.

Went to meet someone but my bad luck is not leaving me,

I have started talking alone in the night because now there is a shortage of those who talk.

Now this tongue does not want to say anything because the listeners have made a distance from me,

Now I have got a reason not to live.

Now I'm a little scared to make eye contact with myself,

Because those who encouraged me have left me alone.

Know what has happened, what has made me alienated from myself,

I have stopped smiling now because those who saw me smiling have turned their backs on me.

Now this life has become colourless,

Because I have found a reason not to live.

My heart is now attached to the darkness,

Because those who took me into the light have now given up their say.

I don't like to go out now,

Because I can't answer any questions to anyone.

How can I tell what is happening to me,

Now I have got a reason not to live.

Now these circumstances have turned against me and feet have started getting tired in the way,

Now I have started getting hurt a bit because the healers are no longer with us.

Now this time is not passing,

Because those who give me time have turned away from me.

Now it has become a habit to walk alone,

Because I have found a reason not to live.

Whom should I call my own, with whom should I keep distance,

I got so much pain from my loved ones that's why I have stopped expecting anything from others.

Loneliness has caught me,

Because the hands that meet with happiness have kept distance from me.

Now this life is afraid to call me my own,

Now I have got a reason not to live.

Poem-4 My life incomplete, now going into loneliness.

It's not easy but I'm trying,

I have not lost from life I have lost from myself.

I feel incomplete even after completing,

I am not saying anything, I am sitting somewhere lost.

It's not a big deal, but it's not worth forgetting,

My life incomplete, now going into loneliness.

I had gone to fight with time,

Now I am feeling defeated.

Wanted to be someone,

Now I'm scared to be myself.

There is no memory of anyone in the eyes now,

My life incomplete, now going into loneliness.

Wanted to come near to others - now I am afraid to come near myself,

I wanted in the morning, now I am crying in the night.

Now there is nothing to complain about,

There is no freshness in my world anymore.

I am getting a little angry with myself now.

My life incomplete, now going into loneliness.

Now the lines have started to fade away,

Yes, my loneliness is eating me up.

The mind has stopped thinking now,

I have to live every moment alone now.

Now I can't see with my own eyes,

My life incomplete, now going into loneliness.

Nowadays, I do not feel this morning as my own,

My closeness is increasing since nights.

Now I don't feel well

Now I don't talk to myself.

Many things are happening to me due to loneliness,

My life incomplete, now going into loneliness.

The night has become its own, now every memory of it is being erased,

Have some faith in myself, I will take care of everything.

I have become a little different from myself now,

Now I have to increase my closeness with myself.

Now his memories are fading from my memories,

My life incomplete, now going into loneliness.

POEM-5 The fate of both of us is not related to each other.

For the first time I told someone my own,

I had a golden dream with you.

Don't know where, what went wrong,

Where I did not like to walk without you Today I have to walk alone.

I tried a lot to be yours,

But maybe the fate of both of us is not related to each other.

Now I feel alone,

You are not near but still I keep talking about you.

It's good that had to happen-happened soon,

Otherwise, if you become my habit, then it will be difficult to live again.

I asked for you in my prayers, you also prayed for thousands,

But maybe the fate of both of us is not related to each other.

Now I have stopped fighting for you with others,

Because to save from the front - now you are not with me.

I was starting to feel strong with you,

Now I have become weak even after being strong alone.

Everyone started liking you and my pair,

But maybe the fate of both of us is not linked to each other.

Eyes tell me to sleep but without you my sleep is lost,

Everything happened so quickly that it would take me some time to meet the truth.

Earlier, I used to find you with me often,

But now my whole day is being spent in remembering you.

With each other we had made our laughter life,

But maybe the fate of both of us is not linked to each other.

There was a moment when I couldn't get tired of taking your name,

Now there is a moment when I am calling you but you do not listen.

There was a moment where I used to see you near me,

Now there is a moment in which I am looking at you but you are not seeing me.

How well we had made each other our own,

But maybe the fate of both of us is not linked to each other.

I will always remember all the things done to you,

No matter how far you go - but your knock will always be there in my memory.

Whatever promises we made to each other,

You do not have them but I will continue to fulfil them.

Now I don't like this world without you

But maybe the fate of both of us is not related to each other.

POEM-6 I will still be incomplete.

I will take myself to say,

I will resort to a little lie - I will console myself a little.

I will forget everything in some time,

Even knowing you - I will refuse to recognize you.

After some time I will move ahead in life,

But without you I will still be incomplete.

Nothing is too hard to say,

But it is not easy to forget someone forever.

I don't know how can I forget you,

But while living in the world, I cannot run away from the truth.

Now I will get used to living without you,

But without you I will still be incomplete.

Now I have to stop going out for a while,

Because everything outside will remind me of you.

I am not so weak that I will be lost in the house forever,

But because I want to forget you forever, it will take some time.

I will tell myself happy now,

But without you I will still be incomplete.

I will take away all your things from me now.

I will burn all your memories with me with my hands.

Now your feeling will not remain anywhere.

From now on - I will not call you my own.

I know it is not easy to live without you now,

But without you I will still be incomplete

I did not have this much right - but still I ask you for a promise,

Whenever both of us passed through a path - then consider me unknown.

One promise will always be mine to you,

I will never talk to you again in life.

Now without you we will get used to being happy,

But without you I will still be incomplete.

57

I am not used to talking much, so I may not have told some things,

But now it doesn't matter if you know these things or not.

I know one thing, I will not be able to forget you,

Still, I have gone out by lying to myself - maybe I can forget you.

To say, there will always be laughter and laughter with everyone,

But without you I will still be incomplete

Poem-7. Forget you.

Tried a lot but it was not possible,

Wanted to erase your name from my mind but I could not.

What was my wish I had decorated my own dream with you,

Wanted to keep you in my eyes – just wanted to be yours.

I remember how easily you told me to forget me - tried a lot,

But the regret is that it was not possible to forget you.

After a long time saw you yesterday - wanted to call you but my family was with me,

When you alone made me - then this family had absorbed me.

I had always dreamed of spending life with you,

But it seems that something is missing - that's why this dream remained only a dream.

I am here, you are somewhere else - both are trying to forget their yesterday in life,

But it is unfortunate that it has never been possible for us to forget you.

Now I am afraid to remember your memories again,

Because if I remember you, I will sit by deceiving myself.

Wherever you are, but I know so much that you must have earned your living,

But what should I do because if I fight to get you back I will lose my loved one.

Made many promises to each other, which I often wanted to forget,

But it was a shame that it was not possible for us to forget you with those promises of yours.

Maybe you do not know that even today when I see you with someone,

I start seeing you with me.

I know these things don't make any sense now,

I understand myself, but this heart does not accept it.

I have already erased all the memories spent with you,

But it was not possible for us to forget everything about you.

I have lived life without you too,

I have come enough ahead, now I have

lost the courage to go back.

If you went, then I also got someone's support,

He taught me the meaning of living life.

Trying to forget you in the midst of many new memories -
the memories have disappeared,

But why was it not possible to forget you?

Listen, whatever happened now happened,

Now I want to live happily for the time to come.

Maybe it is not so easy for me to forget you,

But now I have to take care of my loved ones.

I'm trying to forget you too

But it was not possible to get you out of this heart.

POEM-8 I have to complete the journey ahead without you.

How can I fix the broken relationship now?

The one I was trying for doesn't like being with us anymore.

Don't know what to say - Life doesn't like our relationship or they don't want to be ours,

What a strange game life has played.

Maybe our relationship was up to this point,

Now I have to complete the journey ahead without you.

Will say even from the heart, now you will not even remember them,

Because any of her memories will no longer be with us.

Now the habit of her message or call in the morning will have to be separated from us,

Because now the companion who talks to me is not mine.

Now I have to go on a journey again on a new path of life alone,

Now I have to complete the journey ahead without you.

It was sad for a long time that you made me alone,

But now the heart does not care about loneliness.

I had a relationship with you but you

didn't understand the importance of the relationship,

I had understood you as my own but you never understood us as yours.

Now I have to break the relationship with your life,

Now I have to complete the journey ahead without you.

I started feeling good with you,

I wanted to be a part of your every moment.

It seems that I have taken you too much as my own,

That's why as soon as you knew the time, you made me alone.

I could not be yours - now I have to accept this truth also,

Now I have to complete the journey ahead without you.

I still want to call you mine,

I want to put you in front of my eyes.

Never thought - I will be so separated from you,

I will remember you but I will not be able to see you near me.

Now I have to live by myself for the moment,

Now I have to complete the journey ahead without you.

Till yesterday I used to feel empty every day without you,

Now the same emptiness is calling me its own.

I wanted to make the moment of life beautiful with you,

Now every moment I am feeling only you.

Now I have to get your name out of my mind,

Now I have to complete the journey ahead without you.

Part-3. Poem dedicated to motivation.

POEM-1 This is what I have promised myself.

Only a little time has changed,

I just got a little pain.

Luck has changed a bit,

Life has just changed its course.

I know myself only a little,

Now every experience has to be met.

I have to reach every height of the floor,

This is what I have promised myself.

The light of the eyes has dimmed a little,

But the fire is still burning in my heart.

The paths have become a little long,

But the hope of getting it is also very long.

Still have to deal with the dangers a little more,

I have yet to meet my every failure.

I just got a get tired,

This is what I have promised myself.

No matter how long it takes me,

No matter how difficult the path to the floors may be.

No matter how low the brightness of the hands,

Even if I get hurt.

So far, I have defeated only a few,

I have yet to win by myself.

Now I have to go through every path,

This is what I have promised myself.

Nothing happened yet,

I have yet to meet many more accidents.

I'm missing out right now,

Because just now I have found something difficult.

Have just seen a dream,

Success is yet to be lived.

Now I have to fight with every difficulty,

This is what I have promised myself.

Now only a little has been tolerated,

I have a lot to bear now.

Just walked alone for a few days,

Still have to walk alone for a long time.

Till now I had got everyone's support,

Now I have to walk helpless.

I have to cross every path alone,

This is what I have promised myself.

Right now every moment of mine has been spent in sorrow,

Now I have to wake up at night.

Accidents have happened only a few times,

All the accidents have yet to be met.

I've only walked a few steps now,

There is still a long way to go.

Now I have to paint a little more in the colour of success,

This is what I have promised myself.

POEM-2 I will fulfil my every purpose.

Just a few moments and just a few steps away,

Just a short distance away I have to cross the path now.

I have to fulfil the promise I have made to myself,

I cannot sit with my hand on my hand.

If I lose, how will I make eye contact with myself?

Just for a while, I will fulfil my every purpose.

Now halfway through, I can't turn back,

I can't take my steps back now.

Now I can't give up by coming here,

I did not come this far to see the face of defeat.

Now I will not regret myself after losing,

Just for a while, I will fulfil my every purpose.

I will not wait for the time to change,

I will show my every dream by living it now.

Now I will give all my efforts in my work,

Now I will fulfil the dream which I have filled in my eyes.

Now I will walk every path of my dreams,

Just for a while, I will fulfil my every purpose.

Now it is necessary for me to live every moment,

I want to live my dream soon.

I may be a little tired in the meantime,

But I have to remove every fatigue soon.

Maybe I will take some more time to fulfil my dream,

Just for a while, I will fulfil my every purpose.

I want to believe in myself,

Right now I have to cross a lot of obstacles.

I have to keep the courage on myself,

Now I have to show myself by winning.

I will never give myself the right to lose,

Just for a while, I will fulfil my every purpose.

I want to get myself to my destination,

I want to see myself living my dream.

I will also fulfil my every dream,

For which I will take steps from today and from now on.

Have faith in myself, I will do everything,

Just for a while, I will fulfil my every purpose.

POEM-3 I will walk a little all the time.

It'll take time - I'll have to get tired a bit,

Today I will try again.

I will not let myself be defeated like this,

I will keep encouraging myself.

Not much, I will walk a little all the time.

Even if the destination is a little far away,

No matter how many roads are full of difficulties.

I will meet every difficulty of the destination,

I will not put too much burden on myself.

Not much, I will walk a little all the time.

Some dreams are kept in my eyes,

I have made many promises to myself.

Now even after being far away I do not have to take my steps back,

Now every day I will learn something new.

Not much, I will walk a little all the time.

Mind is saying give yourself rest,

But the heart is saying - Raise yourself in the eyes.

I will reach the destination for myself not for others,

Every moment I will encourage myself to move forward.

Not much, I will walk a little all the time.

Now there is only a short distance left,

The road is running out.

Just a few steps away-my destination is standing nearby,

I will accept it only after getting my destination.

Not much, I will walk a little all the time.

There is a strange feeling in my mind,

I have come this far-the same thing is happening to myself
now.

Don't know how I did it-I don't know how it happened,

I will see myself on the floor now.

Not much, I will walk a little all the time.

POEM-4 I cannot accept defeat like this

Now let's go back - why tiring myself,

Ever since I have listened to the heart - the mind is talking like this.

It's just enough - just done enough,

The foot has also given the same answer.

But I can't leave my dream incomplete like this,

If I have already decided then I cannot accept defeat like this.

Now it's gone a lot - maybe I'm just living in an illusion,

That's why I stand far away even after

walking a long way from success.

Nothing happens if my success is not written in luck now,

I will never lose my courage.

I can't break the promise made to myself to get success like this,

If I have already decided then I cannot accept defeat like this.

It's been a long time following the path chosen for the goal,

Maybe it's not that easy to achieving success.

Maybe it will take a long time,

I just have to wait for some more time to achieve my goal.

No matter how long it takes - I can't take my steps back,

If I have already decided then I cannot accept defeat like this.

I'm just a little tired now,

After some time - I will go again.

Right now - I have just gone through some problems,

In the future I will pass through paths full of difficulties.

I can't be afraid of the problems of a moment,

If I have already decided then I cannot accept defeat like this.

I still have a lot of courage left,

There is still a long way to go in the race.

Don't know what's going to happen next

I just have faith in myself that's why there is life in these feet.

Now I can't live without getting the destination,

If I have already decided then I cannot accept defeat like this.

POEM-5 I still have a long way to go.

I might be forgetting something,

I am probably tired of walking alone.

But don't forget why I came out,

I don't want to make myself weak.

I still have a long way to go.

I don't know, whoever I will be successful,

But if I don't do anything, I will die unsuccessfully.

The tears are yet to come in the eyes,

I am yet to meet my success.

Right now - There is only tiredness in the legs,

I still have a long way to go.

I appreciate that moment,

The moment I started on my path of success.

If I didn't take the decision at that moment I might have
been more late,

Then I could hardly come here.

Not in the eyes of others - I have to rise in my own eyes,

I still have a long way to go.

Where have the dreams of the eyes been fulfilled now,

All my dreams are still incomplete.

What I have promised myself now I have to fulfil that too,

I still have a lot to see in life.

Now I have to sigh after reaching the goal,

I still have a long way to go.

Pray I will fulfil my every dream,

Soon I will take restful sleep.

How will I move forward until I walk?

How can I fill peace in my own moments?

I have to overcome my problems too now,

I still have a long way to go.

If you understand stubbornness then I will say stubbornly,

Soon I will see everyone from my destination.

If not today then tomorrow I will fulfil my every dream,

But I will never be afraid of distance and difficulties.

I don't want to pay attention to others,

I still have a long way to go.

POEM-6 I will fulfil my every dream.

I know - nothing is easy here,

It will take time - don't rush.

I have to maintain my spirits - I do not lose faith in myself,

Life is long - I don't want to stop now.

I will take myself out of every situation,

If not today than tomorrow I will fulfil my every dream.

I'm a little tired - I don't pay much attention to that fatigue,

There is a fire in the eyes to achieve success , I don't want to put out that fire.

Now the distance has not left me - I do not be afraid of distance,

The gap is enough now between success and me - I don't want to lose a single moment.

Now I will spend my every moment in fulfilling my dreams,

If not today than tomorrow I will fulfil my every dream.

I didn't come here to give up so far,

Take my steps back - I have not made any such promise to myself.

I have to reach my destination and fulfil my dream,

The happiness that I will get by getting success - I have to feel that happiness.

In every moment - I will reduce my every distance.

If not today than tomorrow, I will fulfil my every dream.

I agree so far I have not been successful,

But it's only taken time - the decision hasn't changed yet.

One day I will follow my success,

One day I will become something in my own eyes.

I will always try to get success,

If not today than tomorrow I will fulfil my every dream.

Believe in myself, I will not give up like this,

I will understand every story - I will live in every moment.

Now I have to take myself to the destination,

I want to make a name for myself.

I will find myself near the destination one day,

If not today than tomorrow I will fulfil my every dream.

What if I lost the first time,

I will definitely try again.

What happened, I'm a little tired,

I'll walk every now and then for a while.

I will make every moment my own,

If not today then tomorrow I will fulfil my every dream.

POEM-7 I still have a lot to learn from life.

Have to fall a little, have to face a little,

Have to go some distance, have to understand a little.

Have to meet many people, have to explain to many people,

I have to rise myself - I have to become my own companion.

There is so much to do in life now,

I still have a lot to learn from life.

Have a little laugh - have to cry a little,

Life is to be lived sorrows have to be said goodbye.

Now I have to overcome every difficulty,

Have to go through all the difficulties now.

I have to keep moving forward by staying alive,

I still have a lot to learn from life.

The time that was lost moving forward,

I want him to live now.

The hunger for success took away the happiness,

I want to feel it now.

I don't have to waste a moment now,

I still have a lot to learn from life.

The other said, it is forbidden to lose here,

Somebody said that your life is useless.

Somebody taunted the whole life,

No one has even called me their own.

Now I have to answer everyone's questions.

I still have a lot to learn from life.

Well, I am a little away from others,

Otherwise, everyone's despair would have killed me.

Doesn't let me do anything - doesn't let me fulfil my dreams,

Just say yourselves - just get yourself done.

Now I have to complete all my work,

I still have a lot to learn from life.

I believe in myself

I will get back my value for every moment.

Whatever time is wasted,

I will live that time again.

I have enough to laugh now,

I still have a lot to learn from life.

POEM-8 But it has to be converted into truth quickly.

Just have to get out,

Now I want to meet all the people.

I want to know myself a little,

I want to understand some others.

A dream is decorated in the eyes,

I want to see that live.

Now it's just a cable dream,

But it has to be converted into truth quickly.

I have started,

I will see the end soon.

I know now I have to fight with a lot of difficulties,

I know I still have to go through a lot of turns.

But have promised to live the dream,

To see myself at my destination.

Now only a dream has been decorated,

But it has to be converted into truth quickly.

I am and my believe,

I have my own side I have my own dream.

These eyes still have a lot to see,

These legs still have a long way to go.

I am thinking how will I do all this,

But believe in myself, I will do everything.

Right now, only a few memories have been included,

But it has to be converted into truth quickly.

I want to win - now I have to prove myself,

I have to walk alone - I have to face alone.

Now I have to make many mornings my own,

Thought there is a lot - but much work has yet to be done.

I will keep fighting with myself,

I will keep comforting myself.

Next, I want to see myself living a dream,

But it has to be converted into truth quickly.

I have to rise in my own eyes,

I just have to show myself by doing something.

I have enough to live now,

Winning from all the difficulties, have to move forward.

I know everything will take time,

But if it starts now, then the dream will be fulfilled soon.

I have considered my every preparation,

But it has to be converted into truth quickly.

Part-4 . Poem dedicated to motivation.

POEM-1 I have to find success in life on my own.

No one will be with me - no one will be near,

I will be and only I will have faith with me.

Everyone will be happy from outside,

No one will be happy at heart.

No matter what happens, I have to support myself.

I have to find success in life on my own.

No one will come to help - no one will tell me the right path considering me as my own,

Everyone will console me but no one will advise me to move forward.

No matter what happens - I have to face every situation myself,

I have to take care of myself.

I'm right every time I have to prove all this,

I have to find success in life on my own.

No one will understand me,

People will talk a lot but I have to silence people with my success.

I have to fight with people's taunts,

I have to go ahead watching everyone.

Looking at my time, I have to follow my every step,

I have to find success in life on my own.

Whatever happens tomorrow, I don't know,

I have to give my hundred percent today.

I don't know what will happen tomorrow

I have to live every day today.

I have to understand everything today

I have to find success in life on my own.

No one will remember me for a long time,

Everyone will ask me if I get success.

Everyone will probably force me to go towards failure,

Everyone will praise me after reaching success.

I will never stop walking with praise,

I have to find success in life on my own.

It will take a long time to achieve success,

But I have to work with patience.

No matter how angry this world gets with me,

I have to be happy with myself.

In the midst of happiness, I have to keep doing my work too,

I have to find success in life on my own.

POEM-2 Will keep me in memories for a few days and then forget.

I am today, do not know whether I will stay tomorrow,

I am alive now, what do I know tomorrow when I will be lost.

Whatever I want to do, I have to do it today,

I have to complete my unfinished work today.

no one will even remember me,

Will keep me in memories for a few days and then forget.

I still have a lot of work left to do,

There is a dearth of time.

I have to leave my image on this world,

I want to spread my memories in this world.

How am I living no one will ask me this,

Will keep me in memories for a few days and then forget.

Who was I, hardly anyone will remember,

But I always want to be recognized by my work.

One day everyone will forget me

Who was I? Everyone will erase me from their mind.

No one would like to keep me in their memories,

Will keep me in memories for a few days and then forget.

Today I am breathing, but cannot say when my breath will stop,

I don't know when my life will end.

I can't waste my time like this,

Whatever it is, I have to find my success soon.

No one will stand by me,

Will keep me in memories for a few days and then forget.

Today's morning is precious to me,

Tomorrow is not known, maybe I will be able to see tomorrow's morning.

I will not sit like this tomorrow,

Whatever I do - I will do it today.

What do I do - no one cares,

Will keep me in memories for a few days and then forget.

95

Whether I live or not, I will be eternally immortal by my work,

I will be recognized by work - I will be remembered by the work I have done.

Tomorrow I may not meet anyone,

But I will stick in everyone's mind.

No one will say their own

Will keep me in memories for a few days and then forget.